Every Christian is  community which tr
Jesus Christ.
His central teachin
"Love your neighbou
We often find this very difficult.
And the reason we can't love others
is because we haven't learned to
love ourselves.
We hurt others because we lack the
proper kind of self-love.
Why is this?
In the following pages we will
follow 'Joe' from cradle to
maturity in search of some insights.

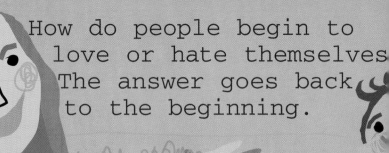

How do people begin to love or hate themselves? The answer goes back to the beginning.

When children are born they are good, beautiful, valuable and loveable.

But they don't know that. They don't know whether they are good or bad, loveable or detestable, superior or inferior.

How do children get to know whether they have worth or not?

2

It is through their relationship with others, and their first contact is with their parents. Normally parents will be the prime influence in forming the child's self-image. Later, come other relationships, teachers, T.V... but first are their parents.

3

A baby is born "brand new" into the world. It is only through contact with others that a child learns their 'value' or otherwise.

When children are loved, prized for themselves, when mother hugs and smiles at them, they feel accepted, wanted, valued ...

But when childhood is without affection and parents' re-actions are of irritation, the child begins to feel insecure. The child wonders..

"Am I bad?"

"Do I cause them to be unhappy?"

"Does she hate me?"

4

Later...

The child beginning to talk and understand, growing in a loving setting will hear things like...

"Joe, you are a good boy."

"Joe I love you."

These kind of things often repeated have a marked effect on Joe...

"I am good and loveable; I am worth something."

5

The way we are treated in our earliest year
influences our ideas about ourselves.
Unconditional love makes us feel worthwhile

But sometimes the love we receive is conditional...

 "Why can't you be like your brother?"

 "Joe, if you don't stop that I won't love you."

 "If you don't stop being bad, God won't love you."

Joe only feels good, worthwhile and loved if he does something, avoids something or becomes something.

 "You're so sweet, I can't help loving you."

Another form of conditional love is when one or both parents only love the child because of their need and they are starving for love themselves.

 "My son Joe is going to be exactly like me."

 "I gave up everything to be a complete mother to Joe."

7

A child at birth does not know what it is.
A child cannot know its identity - whether he is good or bad, loveable or detestable, worth something or worthless.

But we know from philosophy, science and religion that a child as a human person is a marvellous, good and beautiful creature.

The child has an intellect, free will, uniqueness, the power of love, creativity.

And the child is created in the image of God. Jesus Christ, by his birth, gave every child dignity and by his resurrection gave every child future glory.

The child is a diamond - good, loved and made loveable by God himself.

It is through the reflection of himself in the mirror of other people's reactions and attitudes towards the child that he will see, judge, evaluate and thereby come to love or hate himself.

God put in us an unquenchable desire to love and be loved. The human heart cannot long endure a condition of not being loved. Feeling unloved takes away joy, peace, balance. It brings anxiety, conflict and frustration through failure to fulfil the love-winning conditions imposed upon us.

Joe, because he feels loved conditionally and not for his own sake, now feels miserable.

Because he cannot love himself as he is, Joe tries to do everything he feels necessary to win love and acceptance.

When Joe looks at himself now he sees only faults and weaknesses which keep him from winning the conditional love offered him. But he finds if he looks for faults in others his own seem less painful.

"Why is Joe such a fault finder?"

He also finds that to admit to any faults or weaknesses tarnishes his self-image, making him feel even less loved and loveable. Out comes the whitewash and the excuses.

"Why isn't Joe more genuine and honest?"

"Why does he lie and make so many excuses?"

10

As we grow as Christians we learn from RE lessons and the Gospels that we are loved and loveable. That is God's plan.

But, as we have seen, so often we experience conditional love - which only makes us feel a failure. Walled up within ourselves we become afraid of love. We refuse to accept it and become unable to communicate well with others.

As he grows older, Joe dare not reveal his inner feelings to others, even close friends.

He has become shy, bottled up in himself. His conversations are impersonal for fear that his "inferior" self be discovered.

"Nice day today."

"Did you see the match yesterday?"

"I see they've invented a new type of aeroplane"

Joe lacks initiative and creativity. Criticism or failure is too painful.

"What a fool you are!"

"Why don't you?"

Joe now feels very sorry for himself which makes him depressed. Somehow self pity makes him feel better.

NB

The isolation of being
afraid to love and
feeling unloved can make us
feel angry when even little
things go wrong. Sometimes
we project this anger onto
others. Perhaps the real
cause is that we cannot
love ourselves. Our Lord
did say,
"Love your neighbour
as yourself."

"Where
were you
yesterday"

Joe is an unhappy young man. But from his earlier experiences he found that perfect observance of rules and laws enabled him to win approval and affection...

"I never miss prayers."

"I always keep the commandments."

Meticulous rule keeping makes Joe feel safer but his inflexibility leads to further isolation.

"I need a girlfriend that's why I'm lonely"

But Joe is a smother-lover able to love only in a jealous possessive way.

"I want you all to myself."

Joe's passionate craving for love and friendship leads to pre-occupation with sexuality. He struggles between temptation and more feelings of failure.

When we put our friends on a pedestal we effectively imprison them in an attempt to capture them with a possessive love. When they fall from that pedestal we feel rejected and frustrated. Our own love was conditional because we have not yet learned how to love ourselves.

Joe feels isolated. And his refusal to get too closely involved with anyone again cuts off all hope of experiencing unconditional love - his only hope of salvation.

He becomes insensitive to correction or even jokes against himself. He lives in a fantasy world in which he is never wrong.

"It's not my fault."

At times Joe, in his dissatisfaction with being himself, tries to imitate a person he admires - a person he would like to be.

18

The lack of unconditional love in our earlier years, coupled with an experience of strictness or domination by our parents, can make us develop avoidance tactics in later life.

To win his parents love and avoid their anger which Joe, rightly or wrongly interpreted as a rejection of himself, has encouraged Joe to adopt a "Mr nice-guy" attitude. He wants to be liked by everyone.

But inside Joe still sees himself as bad and unloveable. He is suspicious and distrustful of himself and he projects these feelings onto others.

 "I've been around, and in general these days, I'm suspicious of people."

Nowadays, Joe also tends to be a hypochondriac. He needs attention and illness can be a way of defending himself from some obligation he fears.

19

A predominant feeling that many of us live with is FEAR. We are afraid to love, afraid to be loved. We are afraid of rejection. Such fears closes our minds to many of the rich experiences life has to offer.

Joe is fearful and so he lives in a rut, in a set pattern of thinking. Insecurity saturates his whole life. "Perfect love drives out fear". But Joe has yet to experience this perfect love.

Parents can help us to experience unconditional love. If they love their children for themselves, and as they are, those children will grow in self-esteem. But Joe's parents would have liked him to be different.

"I wish Joe liked football like me."

"I wish Joe was brighter."

Joe's parents may not have been at fault. They were influenced by their own upbringing. They may be insecure themselves and unable to love They were simply doing what others did to them.

Feeling unloved makes us feel insecure. We become more concerned about money, status and luxuries. Joe has already become very pre-occupied about his outward appearance.

"Am I too fat?"

"I shall start body building."

21

We often reach mid-life before we begin to question what our life is all about and think about the kind of people we have become. Sometimes it takes a serious crisis in our lives to make us take a fresh look at ourselves.

Joe's life till now...

Joe was born unique, precious and a miracle of God's creative love but he doesn't know it.

He got to know himself and his worth by seeing himself in the reflection of the mirrors of other people's reactions to him, especially those of his parents.

When he was loved for himself he sparkled. But all too often the love he received was conditional on fulfilling certain expectations. He believes that to gain love and worth he must satisfy the demands of others. He has stopped being himself. And he has tried to re-fashion himself into a love-winning image.

He cannot fulfil all the conditions and so he experiences conflict, fear, frustration and anxiety.

"Snap out of it Joe."

Nearly all our difficulties in trying to be genuine Christians and loving children of God stem from our lack of self-love. We devalue ourselves and so build up defence mechanisms which are self-destructive. Often we cannot see the damage this lack of self-love causes.

"My trouble is, I love myself too much."

"Whatever I try, I still seem to get no better as a Christian."

24

"You ought to do this then this"

"You're making a mountain out of it."

"I want to improve but I can't go on much longer. I'm near breaking point. But no-one seems to understand."

"If only I could start again, be born again. If I could start afresh in a different atmosphere maybe things would change."

Sometimes Joe tries to speak to someone…

"Snap out of it Joe."

"You're making a mountain out of it."

"You ought to do this, then this."

In order to become fully alive, fully human, and as God intended, we each need to find someone in life who has an 'UNDERSTANDING HEART', who will help us look at ourselves as we really are - good points and bad points. We also need to learn to become 'UNDERSTANDING HEARTS' ourselves.

Joe's loneliness, fear and despair is destroying him. He feels no-one understands him. He needs help.

"I feel miserable, ready to give up. I'm a mess."

Joe senses someone who might help. He edges in carefully, afraid that he may be attacked. Little by little he tests for negative reactions.

Joe gradually begins to describe his feelings and his faults.

The UH does not judge or reprimand, not console, analyse, agree or disagree.
Joe's troubles are not diagnosed and no easy solutions are suggested.

"I've never been able to tell anyone this before."

The UH does not reject, threaten, attack or apply pressure. The UH is not even trying to change Joe, but simply accepts him as he is - unconditionally. Joe begins to feel free. The UH is an intent, sensitive listener.

"I can begin to see clearly now. It's like having a mirror reflecting my thoughts and feelings. I'm beginning to find my real self. I can see more clearly."

27

Often, when we try to work out our problems or anxieties on our own we find we are in a fog - a fog of emotions. We are too close to ourselves to see clearly. When we find someone we can be totally open and honest with, we see ourselves in the reflection of their kindness. Such an understanding heart helps us to drop the false fronts and roles we play in order to cope with life. We begin to be free to be ourselves.

Joe realises that most of his life has been determined by his desire to respond to the demands of others.

"I'm always trying to think or feel how other people expect me to!" "I have never been totally honest with myself."

Joe realises that he is hardly ever himself because he is a slave to what others think. But the UH has helped him to look at himself with freedom.

"I can see now why life has been such a struggle. I must start to become myself."

Joe is "being born again". Because he has experienced love without any conditions attached he has a second chance to grow and mature.

Joe begins to grow. Not by systematically rooting out faults but through love which makes him aware that his defence mechanisms - his faults - are useless and self-destroying. He learns to accept himself as he is, and in turn begins to become an UH to others.

"Yes, he
always seems
to understand
without making
you feel bad."

Once we accept ourselves as
we are and as of value
because we are God's unique
creation, we begin to love
ourselves unconditionally.
In turn we begin to radiate
this kind of love to others.

The more Joe accepts himself, the more
he accepts and loves others as they are.

"Yes, he always seems to
understand without making
you feel bad."

"Joe is so kind."

"Joe is so kind."

To accept ourselves is not simply a grudging or reluctance acceptance, it is a growing to like ourselves. And to like ourselves doesn't mean we become conceited or self-assertive. Joe now finds a quiet pleasure in being himself.

Jesus said, "Love your neighbour as yourself". As Christians we must try to be patient and forgiving towards our neighbour. That means we must also try to treat ourselves in that way. Jesus also said, "Thou shall not kill". Joe was destroying himself before with hatred.

"I used to think I was a worthless sinful creature, beyond saving."

"I was full of self-hatred."

31

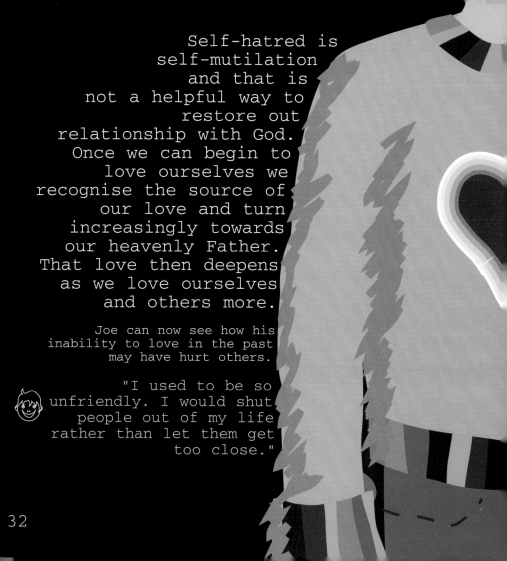

Self-hatred is self-mutilation and that is not a helpful way to restore out relationship with God. Once we can begin to love ourselves we recognise the source of our love and turn increasingly towards our heavenly Father. That love then deepens as we love ourselves and others more.

Joe can now see how his inability to love in the past may have hurt others.

"I used to be so unfriendly. I would shut people out of my life rather than let them get too close."

32

He discovers that the more he learns to love other people, the more he discovers himself and his own personality.

"I never realised I had this gift of making people feel at ease."

The real test of whether we love ourselves is the way we react when we fall into sin. Joe used to experience long moods of guilt, especially if the sin were associated with sexuality or uncharitableness.

Joe used to think that these moods were feelings of sorrow for his sins. Now he knows that much of it was obsessive guilt. He no longer lets himself get low and miserable for days, thereby hating himself and others. Instead he seeks God's forgiveness, forgives himself and learns a little more about unconditional love.

"I understand, don't let it get you down."

It is a sad fact that many people, even Christians, imagine God as a tyrant who only loves people who fit into a certain mould. God loves each one of us as we are and regardless of our faults and failings. That is unconditional love.

Joe is learning to be patient with his own faults and those of others. He knows that this is the way to let them know that his love is genuine and sincere.

"Let me help you?"

Joe realises too, that although many actions appear sinful and malicious on the surface, they are often coloured by human weakness and vulnerability.

"I remember I used to be so unkind to Mrs Smith. It was as though I didn't have to look at own faults then."

Nowadays, Joe has got a very UH.

"All who believe in Jesus will have their sins forgiven."

Does learning to forgive ourselves and others mean that we become so relaxed and easy-going about our faith that we simply resemble a contented cow or a sack of potatoes? Is that what maturity means?

Before Joe became the man he is now, he already had a deep appreciation of the nature of suffering.

"I firmly believe in Christ's passion, death and resurrection."

Joe knew, too, that the Holy Spirit could and did inspire and sanctify him even in his weakness.

"When I am weak, them I am strong." St Paul.

Joe knows that suffering is precious when united with that of Christ. He wants his suffering to stem not from turning in on himself, but from going out and relating to others.

"My calvary now is to try to accept others as they are. I want to gain greater freedom in loving that way."

The end result is that Joe suffers more. It hurts to put ourselves out by getting involved with others: we have to die each day, emptying ourselves of our feelings in order to feel with others.

"Loving is a risky business."

"Its hard to love Fred."

37

Unlike us, God does not love because he needs something. He has everything. That's why his love is totally giving, creative love.

Now confident of his own loveability,
Joe has become less defensive.
He realises that criticism towards him is not
always a personal attack but maybe a sign that
the other person is in need of love.

Joe feels freer to wander into any group and to
face anyone, however hostile. He has discovered
that unconditional love disarms others.

Christ's life showed us the completeness of his
Father's unconditional love in his love for
sinners. Joe understands this now that he is
trying to live in the same way.

39

From his own experience Joe has learned
a lot about human nature. As a result
of his encounters with understanding
hearts, his attitude towards people
has changed a lot.

Joe used to try to change others. He would point out their
faults, tell them off or ridicule them.

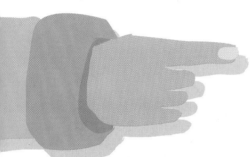

"You really should try
to give that up!"

In more subtle ways, too, he tried to manipulate people by
making comparisons or joking about their shortcomings.

Joe used to think he could change people by simply telling
them what they ought or ought not to do. He overlooked
their feelings.

The real problems are people's feelings: feelings of fear,
self-hatred or feeling unloved. Joe realises now that
people usually know already what's wrong with them; to
tell them only increases their problems.

We have seen that many of our faults stem from symptoms of deeper ailments within ourselves. How can we create a safe atmosphere in which we can dispense with the need to be defensive, make excuses or play a role?

These days Joe wants people to be able to be themselves when they are with him; he wants them to know he cares about them as they are with both good and bad points.

"What do you think?"

How can Joe convey this in a practical way?

He recalls that the cause of his earlier difficulties was the absence of unconditional love in his life; when he received it, he learned to accept himself. These were the two key points.

"I will accept people as they are."

"I will not try to change them."

Joe's approach to other's becomes one of sincere love and understanding. He finds people begin to change spontaneously in this atmosphere - they start to become the people that God created them to be.

44

Once we really and truly accept a person as he or she is and communicate that acceptance to them, he or she begins to change.

Joe doesn't become 100% permissive in that he never advises or reprimands when in a position of authority. But because he has communicated an understanding attitude people accept that he is not attacking or rejecting them as persons.

"I know you've done your best but let's look at it again."

Joe knows that people generally are sensitive and defensive, afraid to be themselves in case they are rejected or disliked. So Joe tries to avoid arousing defences in people, he doesn't want to hurt them.

"I understand..."

Joe remembers how he used to be 10-15 years ago. He knows some people still see him as that kind of person.

"Joe has always been a show off."

Joe can see that he and others have changed a lot over the years. He recognises that it's wrong to categorise people once and for all and to treat them according to the label which has been given to them.

Our task is not to evaluate people but to understand them.

It is a great source of peace for Joe to realise that it is not necessary for him to try to change people or to judge them.

He has learned that interpreting or analysing another's life is too big a responsibility for him or anyone else. Nor is it possible. Everyone is unique.

Joe no longer feels an obligation to make a happy ending to every problem by solving it himself.

"I don't really know."

When people come to him for help, Joe concentrates on them as individuals rather than focussing on their problems.

"This person is capable, only fear and mistrust will hold him back."

It may seem that we have followed Joe
rather rapidly through change to a sudden,
happy ending. But such change in reality is
very slow and gradual.

Although Joe has experienced new insights and changing attitudes, he still has many faults.

"I feel low so I'm not going to bother too much with anyone today."

Though inclined to be independent and exclusive, Joe does appreciate the need for community and togetherness especially in Church.

Joe has learned that he grows best in deep personal relationships. These relationships depend on receptivity and honesty.

Before Joe met an **UH**, he was closed in on himself, he could not relate well to people. But having received unconditional love he began to have faith in love and develop a taste for it.

"Now I find I trust people more and I have more friends."

"Now I find I trust people more and I have more friends."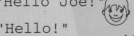

"Hello Joe!"

"Hello!"

49

Once we feel at ease about loving ourselves we become more receptive to the idea of loving others unconditionally - we become more open.

Our parable of Joe and the UH gives us a fascinating insight into divine grace and how it works. Grace is the relationship of love which exists between God and his children.

Grace is not something which is superimposed upon us like a rubber stamp.

It interacts with our nature. Therefore the more we know about interpersonal relationships - what love does to people - the more we know about Divine grace.

51